THE ESSENTIAL BOOK OF

CRYSTAL
HEALING

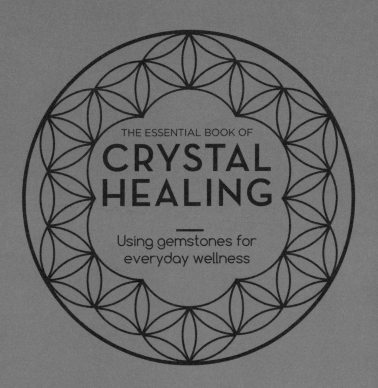

THE ESSENTIAL BOOK OF

CRYSTAL HEALING

Using gemstones for
everyday wellness

SUZANNE EDWARDS

SIRIUS

SIRIUS

This edition published in 2023 by Sirius Publishing, a division of Arcturus Publishing Limited,
26/27 Bickels Yard, 151–153 Bermondsey Street,
London SE1 3HA

ISBN: 978-1-3988-3011-0
AD010567UK

Printed in China

Contents

Notes on safety and ethics

SAFELY USING CRYSTALS

Crystals are powerful tools and allies. They are potent healing materials at our disposal. They are also extremely beautiful. It is tempting to cover ourselves and our homes in hundreds of stones. Of course, we have to decide for ourselves how we want to work with them, but we may not reap the maximum benefit by using them in this way.

Imagine going to the doctor and being given 20 different medicines. One, or perhaps two, are likely to be more effective. Our bodies can get overloaded and confused by so many different energies. When working with crystals, I recommend you allow time for the work you have done to sink in and integrate, before trying too many different practices or stones.

If you decide to wear stones, especially if you desire a specific healing or outcome, I recommend wearing one stone—or, at most, two different stones. This focuses your intent and can make for a more effective result.

If you have a serious medical condition, such as cancer or heart problems, you might want to use stones sparingly. Remember that the stones are stimulating and activating our chakras and recognize that moderation can be more healing.

It is important to remember that crystals are not a substitute for seeking professional medical advice.

THE CRYSTAL INDUSTRY AND ETHICS

Interest in crystals has been big business for many years but the past ten years have seen an even bigger boom. Some mining practices are environmentally and ethically dubious, the miners exploited and working in terrible conditions. Indeed, certain mining areas in the world fund and fuel war. You should check the companies you buy from to find out their standards and policies on sourcing.

Introduction

Crystals have dazzled and amazed throughout the ages. There is something about their shapes and colours that emanate magic and wonder. Many a crystal fan will attest to being "like a kid in a sweetshop" when faced with a shop or fayre full of crystals.

They have been the source of make-believe in many films. Think of the fantasy classic *The Dark Crystal*, and two *Indiana Jones* films: *The Kingdom of the Crystal Skull* and *The Temple of Doom* (which features Shiva lingams). Even though these are fictional fantasy films, they still impart the feeling that crystals have the potential to wield immense, otherworldly power, either for good or for selfish, destructive gain.

Crystals have been (and are) used by mystics and scientists alike. Prepare yourself for a magical adventure into the crystalline universe!

CHAPTER 1
How does crystal healing work?

Crystals have been valued by humans for millennia – and are much older than humanity itself. The oldest, still-intact crystal is about 4.4 billion years old, and formed when the Earth had cooled, after its formation about 4.56 billion years ago.

Throughout time and across cultures, humans have believed that crystals hold magical and healing properties. There are records of crystals for use in healing in Indian, Chinese and Egyptians scriptures. The first documented reference to use of crystals was with the Sumerians around in 4000 BCE. They were a people who lived in the region currently known as Iraq, who used crystals in magical incantations. There were also malachite mines in Sinai from 4000 BCE.

The Egyptians viewed lapis lazuli as representative of the cosmic bodies of the sky and the stars: the goddesses Nuit and Maat. It was associated with higher wisdom, and Queen Cleopatra crushed it up for eyeshadow. Dancers would adorn themselves with ruby and carnelian, often worn in the navel. These crystals were believed to enhance sexual magnetism. Some of the rooms in the pyramids and temples had features made from quartz, while others have crystal plinths that are said to have been used for healing. There are also theories that some of the chambers in the pyramids were specifically built to vibrate at certain frequencies to heal organs and different parts of the body. It is possible that the Egyptians had knowledge of healing using crystals combined with sound.

Crystals have an important place in shamanic cultures, where they are seen as objects of power. In Native American traditions, beliefs about the roles of crystals vary between the different tribes and regions, but crystals are generally referred to as the Stone People, and seen as living sentient beings that are capable of communication with those who can hear them and who are willing to listen. They are record keepers, holding the history of Mother Earth, and the deliverers of her messages.

In Cherokee culture, each person owned a crystal. When that person passed over, it was inherited by a son or daughter. They could use it to communicate with that person in a time of need. These crystals were a vital link for the ancestors, and between the living and dead. They were also used to assist with hunting.

The Huichols of Mexico viewed quartz as the crystallized souls of dead shamans. The Ancient Greeks called quartz *krustallos*, believing it was a form of supercooled ice.

The tradition of using crystals in India is unbroken to this day, and runs alongside modern medicine.

The New Age movement, whose ideas were introduced by Madame Blavatsky in the late 1800s, popularized crystal healing as we know it today. That movement became more visible in the 1970s.

The continent of Atlantis, made up of several islands, is a feature of New Age beliefs. It may have been a real place, which is now submerged somewhere in the Atlantic Ocean. According to New Age beliefs, the Atlanteans were an extremely advanced civilization that had technology comparable to what we have today, psychic abilities and a sophisticated knowledge of how to heal with crystals. Some posit that many of the Atlanteans used their knowledge for greed, however, and ended up destroying themselves and sinking the islands.

Nikola Tesla, the scientist who helped to design AC (the alternating current of the modern electricity supply system), had a strong interest in crystals. A charge of electricity can be released through crystals, and in 1900 Tesla said: "In a crystal we have clear evidence of a formative life principle, and though we cannot understand the life of a crystal, it is nonetheless a living being."

In present times, crystals are used in all sorts of technology:

some lasers use rubies, while mobile phones, computers and watches contain quartz. Some water filters contain shungite. Beauty companies have even taken their cue from the ancient Egyptians and use rose quartz in their products. Diamonds are also extremely suitable for high-power electronics, being the ultimate semiconductor, and their use may become more prevalent in the future.

How does it work?

There is no absolute explanation as to how or why healing with crystals and gemstones works. It may be because we have crystals inside us — particularly our bones, which contain quartz. We are also composed of minerals and a certain intake is necessary for us to function well. Gemstones contain various minerals, and when worn next to the skin are said to infuse the bloodstream with minerals to create certain healing effects. This explanation has been questioned, though, because many stones are insoluble. Nonetheless, bloodstone contains iron and is said to fortify the blood, especially when worn next to the skin. And it should be noted that bracelets made of copper are popular for people with arthritis.

A possible explanation for the healing capabilities is that of energetic resonance. When they are cleansed and charged, crystals carry highly charged vibrational energy, comparable to electricity. When a person is sick, depleted or not in an optimum emotional or mental state, the crystal can shift the person's energy via the process of energetic entrainment to a more harmonious frequency to match its own. Thus, the person feels better afterwards. Imagine a crystal being like a mentor who teaches and guides you to do things more effectively and helps you to elevate your consciousness. After time in their company, you are uplifted. This effect might not last forever, but repeated sessions with either the same teacher or different ones may let you accomplish a more lasting effect. The reason is down to our own crystalline structures and how we respond to them.

It is possible to charge and programme crystals, a bit like batteries. They can absorb and emit energy. There are different opinions about this. Some say that they are indiscriminate and will take on any type of programming that you put in them. Others say that they are sentient beings that may have a specific purpose or preference, and that it is respectful to tune into them to check. This is something that you can explore and decide upon yourself with your own experiences.

Crystals also activate the chakras (energy centres), which we will explore further in Chapter 3. They can activate and boost the energy in these centres and absorb excess energy, harmonizing and rebooting our energy system.

Crystals are also living beings with their own spirit. So, not only are we connected to their physical properties but there is also a spirit inside each stone with powerful capabilities to connect us to different spiritual beings and dimensions beyond time and space.

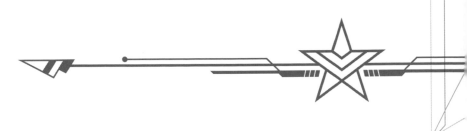

CHAPTER 2
Choosing, cleansing, charging and programming crystals

Choosing

There is such a plethora of crystals, it can seem overwhelming to know where to start. So perhaps first ask yourself, what do you want to use them for? Is it just general curiosity and attraction at this stage? Do you want one to wear? Or do you want to heal something specific?

If it's for general curiosity and attraction or jewellery, I suggest following your intuition. Many humans will automatically go on visual attraction, and although this is important, it can be good to hold them and feel their vibration, especially because they emit a frequency. If you are in a shop or at a stall, bear in mind, though, that they may have been handled by many people, so you could be picking up on other peoples' vibrations. A quick tip for cleansing them there and then is to hold it cupped with both hands and visualize sending white light from the palms of your hands into the crystal, clearing it. Then hold it between your hands or even against your stomach to feel how its vibration merges with yours.

There are two ways that you can approach this: either go for the one that feels the most pleasurable or the one that feels unpleasant.

The latter might sound strange, but it is highlighting an imbalance inside you, which means this stone could be an effective healer for you.

When crystals/gemstones are set in metal for jewellery, the metal amplifies the effect of the stone.

If you are looking to heal something specific, again I recommend you follow your intuition, but make an intention that you are looking for that specific purpose. There is a list in this book of many crystals and their various known healing qualities, so see if any of those ones attract you.

Throughout this book, we will meet our crystal allies, so take a look and see which of the Stone People pops out at you.

Cleansing

I nterestingly enough, crystals can be cleansed by the same methods we use for ourselves. Since we are partly crystalline, this follows.

WATER

You can run a crystal under a tap. Even better if you have access to a stream or the sea. Take note here that some crystals, such as selenite, are soluble, so are best kept completely away from water. Please check, or your crystal might dissolve!

SMUDGING

This is the practice of passing an object through purifying smoke such as bundles of sage, palo santo wood or resins that are burned on a charcoal disc, like copal or frankincense. These can be found at most spiritual shops.

SOUND

Different types of chimes, bells, singing bowls and tuning forks are brilliant for quickly clearing the energies of crystals. The sound can also charge the stones and further activate their energies. Alternatively, use your voice. Chanting and/or singing tones into the stones will do the job.

BREATH

You can blow on the stone. Visualize that your breath is light, cleaning the stone.

RICE

Take a container of rice and submerge the crystal inside it. Leave it overnight or however long you feel is needed.

Charging

EARTH

Bury the stone in the Earth, preferably outdoors, but if that isn't available to you, bury it in soil in a flowerpot. Leave overnight or even longer if possible.

LIGHT — SUN OR MOON

Leaving crystals out to dry and charge in the sunlight is a great way to charge them, but if they are soluble you don't need to wet them first. Just put in the Sun. Even if just on a windowsill, this will charge them and give them energy. Be aware, though, that some stones might lose their colour, especially those of a lighter colour, so don't leave them for too long.

Leaving stones to charge under moonlight, particularly during the full moon, is a wonderful way to charge them. Don't worry if you don't have a direct connection to full moonlight. Leave them on a windowsill, where they will still pick up on the energies. Even better, if they are not soluble, place them in a glass of milk (any kind) and leave them there overnight.

SOUND

Different forms of sound can clear and charge crystals. If you ever go to a sound bath (a specific event where different healing instruments are used), treat your crystals and take them with you. They will feel very different afterwards.

HEALING ENERGY

If you work with channelling energy through your hands, either naturally or something like Reiki, you can place crystals between your hands to charge them. If this is something unfamiliar to you, you can learn it easily by regular practice of the exercises in Chapter 5.

Programming/ deprogramming

This is where you charge a stone with a specific intention. For instance, you may ask an amethyst stone to give you sweet dreams or a citrine to bring you abundance. Be clear and simple about your intention. This will be more effective.

Consider checking with each stone before use, to confirm that it wants to carry out your intention. You can either do this intuitively or use a pendulum (see below).

To clear the programming, simply use the above methods to cleanse the crystals of the intention you have placed in them, holding in your mind the idea that crystal is being cleaned as you do this.

BLOWING

Blow the intention into the stone while thinking about what you want. I suggest doing this three times.

THIRD EYE

Place the stone at the point between your eyebrows and project your intention into the stone through your third eye.

SPEAK

Say out loud the intention that you are programming into the stone.

CARE

It is very important to regularly cleanse your crystals, even if you are not using them, because they pick up on energies and their energies can be dulled. If they have not been cleansed and you use them, they could end up passing on negative energies instead of healing. Do a cleansing once a month on a full moon.

WHEN A CRYSTAL BREAKS

There is a theory that a crystal breaking means that it has absorbed an intense amount of negative energy and has now sacrificed itself to heal you. (Obviously, it can also break due to an accident or too much heat or water.) When this happens, give the crystal back to the Earth by burying it or putting it in a river or the sea.

Using a pendulum

A pendulum can be a very useful ally when working with crystals. A pendulum is an object hanging from the end of a chain or string and able to swing freely. For our purposes it is normally made from crystal, metal or glass. Most retailers selling crystals will also sell these too. There tends to be quite a range of different pendulums, so again go with your intuition. Try holding different ones to see how they swing and how they feel, then choose the one you prefer.

HOW TO USE A PENDULUM

Hold the pendulum with your active hand
(the one you use for writing).

Ask it to show you a 'Yes'. Wait and watch. It may go in
a circle – note the direction. Or in a line – again, note the
direction.

Ask it to show you a 'No'. It's the same process.

You may find this easy or not; it might take time. Be
patient and persistent with your practice.

> The pendulum is a useful tool for choosing
> crystals and healing tools, finding out which
> chakras need the most attention. In a broader
> sense you can ask about all sorts of things.

Clear your mind by doing a simple meditation before you
use the pendulum so you can be more impartial.

To hone your skills, experiment by asking it different
questions that you don't know the answer to but which
can be found out easily. For instance: *Will it rain today?
Will I receive that parcel today?*

CHAPTER 3
Chakras

Activating and rebalancing the chakras is a big feature in crystal healing, so, an understanding of the chakra system is useful. The word *chakra* comes from the Sanskrit for 'spinning wheel'. Chakras are energetic centres at different points on the body that are said to be spinning vortexes of energy. They can be underactive or overactive. They correlate to different areas in life, to emotions and to specific organs and body parts. When they are out of balance, we can have mental or physical symptoms and discomfort.

There are said to be 114 chakras, though seven are well known. For the purposes of this book, I will focus on 13.

Earth Star chakra

This is located 30–45 cm (12–18 inches) below your feet and roots you to the Earth. It also has connections with your past-life patterns and karma. It allows you to discharge negative and stagnant energies from your auric field into the Earth to be recycled and then draw up fresh, nurturing energy. This is important for releasing electromagnetic smog, to which most of us are constantly exposed. Qigong and Tai Chi practitioners work a lot with this chakra.

An imbalance in this chakra can manifest as feeling ungrounded or unstable in life, and it is also associated with depression, paranoia and delusions, a lack of energy, myalgic encephalomyelitis (ME), problems with blood circulation and hip, knee, leg and ankle pain.

The colours for this chakra are black, brown and blue.

Stones for this chakra: black tourmaline, nuummite, black obsidian, orange kyanite, shungite and smoky quartz. Hematite has a special role in activating this chakra.

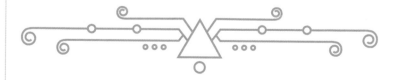

Root chakra

The root chakra is located at the base of the spine, at the tailbone. This also connects you to the Earth and is a grounding chakra. It is about survival instincts – i.e. the basic resources for living, such as food, money and a home – and a sense of safety and belonging. If you have unresolved trauma around these issues, that can manifest as a blockage in the root chakra.

Imbalances can show up as anxiety/fear (especially around money and safety), a lack of energy, scattered thinking, and feeling ungrounded. It is also associated with diarrhoea/constipation, autoimmune diseases, lack of periods, severe lower back pain, bladder problems and arthritis.

The colour for this chakra is red.

Stones for this chakra: obsidian, shungite, black tourmaline, onyx, nuumite, red jasper, garnet, ruby, Shiva lingam, smoky quartz, bloodstone and moss agate.

Sacral chakra

This is located between the belly button and the pubic bone, and is related to sexuality, creativity, pleasure and self-worth. This area is where we hold onto energy from sexual encounters and partners.

When it is out of balance, problems with the urinary tract, reproductive system, PMS, diabetes, lack of or excessive sex drive, impotence, infertility, lower back pain, sexual shame, an inability to flow with life, blocked/suppressed creativity and low self-worth.

The colour for this chakra is orange.

Stones for this chakra: orange kyanite, carnelian, orange calcite, fire opal, red zircon, amber and Shiva lingam.

Solar plexus chakra

This is located in the upper abdomen, around the stomach area. It is linked with personal power, self-esteem and the ability to manifest and make things happen. It is connected to the digestive system.

When imbalanced, it can manifest as problems with digestion, eating disorders, pancreas, stomach ulcers, eczema and gallstones. This can also show as intense emotions that are difficult to 'digest'. It is also associated with a lack of boundaries and taking on too much of other peoples' problems and emotions. This can also manifest in being too domineering or submissive.

The colour for this chakra is yellow.

Stones for this chakra: citrine, tiger's eye, pietersite, yellow apatite, pyrite, fire opal, golden topaz and malachite.

Heart chakra

This is located in the middle of your chest. It is where we relate to others, and it's where we feel love and empathy. It is also said that the soul resides in this centre. It is the midpoint where the lower, more Earthy elements meet the higher centres where we connect with our mind and spirit, ideally, giving a harmonious balance and union.

Imbalances show themselves in heart problems, asthma, chest infections and frozen shoulder. Emotionally this can show as difficulties connecting, being shy and isolated and feeling jealous. It is associated with a tendency to put everyone before yourself, but also an inability to be empathic — depending on how the imbalance manifests.

The colours for this chakra are green and pink.

Stones for this chakra: watermelon tourmaline, ruby, rose quartz, kunzite, rhodonite, rhodocrosite, morganite, aventurine, malachite, emerald and opal.

Throat chakra

This is in the throat, and is associated with communication and personal power. When we have a healthy sense of personal power, we have the ability to speak our truth, express our emotions and communicate information and ideas while at the same time listening to others and hearing what they say — and all of this comes from a balanced throat chakra.

When it is out of balance, we may see problems with the throat, thyroid, gums, teeth, tongue, jaw and sinuses. An imbalance is also associated with ADHD, speech impediment and autism.

The chakra is also associated with difficulty in communication and speaking your mind. Conversely, excessive talking, not being able to listen, lying and insincerity.

The colour for this chakra is blue.

Stones for this chakra: aquamarine, larimar, blue lace agate and lapis lazuli.

Third Eye chakra

This is located between the eyebrows. It relates to intuition, spiritual vision, imagination and the mind. When it is in balance, we have a vision of our life, an ability to see things from a higher perspective, imagination, good cognitive abilities and we are in touch with our intuition.

When it is out of balance, headaches and migraines can occur, as well as hearing and sight problems, ear and eye issues, autism and epilepsy. It is also associated with difficulties with concentration, an overloaded mind, fanatical beliefs, a tendency to take on other peoples' ideas too easily, delusional tendencies, blocked intuition, a lack of vision and narrow-mindedness.

The colour for this chakra is indigo.

Stones for this chakra: lapis lazuli, labradorite, amethyst, tiger's eye, pietersite, opal, fluorite, charoite, iolite and pearl.

Crown chakra

This is situated at the centre of the top of the head. It governs the divine and spiritual connection with 'all that is'. Linked with the brain and the nervous system, it connects you to your purpose. When it is in balance, a person is in a state of bliss.

When out of balance, there will be problems with sleep (either insomnia or excessive sleep) and an extra sensitivity to electromagnetic and environmental energies, and a bombardment of information and messages from spirit. It could also bring out controlling tendencies, close-mindedness and stubbornness.

The colours for this chakra are violet and white.

Stones for this chakra: moonstone, apophyllite, howlite, petalite, selenite, clear calcite, amethyst, lepidolite.

Soul Star Chakra

This is normally situated about 15 cm (6 inches) above the crown of the head. In some cases it can go up to 30–60 cm (12–24 inches).

The Soul Star is where we receive Divine Love. Activating and opening this chakra helps to keep the Crown chakra open and align the seven main chakras. It's also advisable to work with the Earth Star chakra to keep the balance between the higher and lower centres.

The Soul Star chakra connects you with angels and spirit guides. Working with it allows you to clear karma and feel a sense of calm and serenity. When in balance, there is the potential to work towards enlightenment.

When imbalanced, a sense of being lost and without purpose can occur, as well as addictive tendencies, grandiose delusions and an overblown spiritual ego.

The colours of this chakra are luminous white and gold.

Stones for this chakra: amethyst, apophyllite, petalite and selenite. Pyrite has a strong connection with this chakra.

Feet Chakras

There is a chakra on each foot —just slightly under the ball of each foot on the arch. They are really important for grounding us, keeping our connection to the Earth and discharging energy from us and receiving it back into our bodies.

Grounding crystals can be placed under these chakras to activate and heal these chakras. Try hematite, smoky quartz, black tourmaline and red jasper. This can also help with circulation, inflammation and discharging electromagnetic smog.

Hand chakras

These are centred in the middle of our palms and they connect with the heart. They give out and receive energy, much like the feet chakras. If you do any healing and channelling work, it is important to work with these chakras so that you can receive and give out more energy.

Any crystal is suitable for these chakras.

Chakra	Glands	Organs and body parts
Root	Ovaries and Testes	Kidneys, spine and rectum
Sacral	Adrenals	Bladder, kidneys, gall bladder and spleen
Solar Plexus	Pancreas	Intestines, liver, bladder, stomach and upper spine
Heart	Thymus	Heart and lungs
Throat	Thyroid	Bronchial tubes, vocal cords, respiratory system, mouth, tongue and oesophagus
Third eye	Pituitary	Eyes, ears and brain
Crown	Pineal	Spinal column and brain stem

CHAPTER 4
Sensing and harnessing the energy in our hands

Here we can begin to feel energy/chi in our hands, grow our sensitivity to it and learn to expand it. As mentioned before, we are crystalline in part, especially in our bones. We vibrate an electromagnetic frequency that resonates with crystals, and this field can heal both ourselves and others. You need no initiation or attunement to work with it, just a few tips and practice. Think of when you knock yourself on something: often our instinctive reaction is to put our hands on the area to relieve the pain. We are all natural healers.

Learning to harness the energy in our hands is very beneficial when working with crystals, as you will be able to feel and differentiate between their individual energies and sense more easily how they may help you. You will be able to feel when they need charging and cleansing more easily. You will also be able to charge them with your own natural healing energy, and feel what is going on in your own chakras and with other people's.

SENSING HAND ENERGY EXERCISE

Stand or sit in a comfortable position.

Rub the palms of your hands together vigorously for a minute.

Separate your palms a few inches apart.

Feel what you feel:

> Do you feel heat or cold?
> Do you feel tingling?
> Or do you feel that you *see* rather than *feel* something between your hands?

Stay with this for a minute. Then see how far you can expand your hands before you start to lose the sensation.

Repeat this exercise regularly and see how it changes.

With practice you may find that the distance between your hands increases.

Experiment: for instance, see if there's any difference after showering/bathing or between the morning and night-time.

After several weeks of regular practice, try picking up your crystals and placing them between your palms to see if your sensitivity has changed. Or go into a crystal shop and feel different stones.

EXERCISE TO EXPAND AND CONNECT WITH EARTH/COSMIC HEALING ENERGIES

Once you are more comfortable with feeling and expanding your own chi, you can progress to drawing in more energy from the Earth and Cosmos/Sky to heal yourself or others or simply to feel a greater sense of connection.

Sit or stand in a comfortable place. Close your eyes.

Take a moment to get comfortable in your body.

Do a quick body scan to check if you are holding tension anywhere such as your jaw, eyes, neck, shoulders, stomach and hips and then relax those muscles.

Check your posture is straight but not strained.

Feel into the souls of your feet.

Imagine/see/feel that there are roots growing out of the soles of your feet, growing deep down into the Earth.

They grow deeper and deeper into the Earth, penetrating her crust and going deeper still, until they reach the core.

Once you feel they have reached the core, take a few breaths in and out of the roots.

Feel that you are drawing the Earth's energy up into your body. As you breathe out, feel that you are releasing any stagnant, toxic energy and emotions back into her.

Take some time here.

When you are ready, bring your attention up from your feet to the crown of your head.

Sense/see that up, far in the heavens, is a star that is personal to you.

Once you feel a connection, shoot a silver cord up to the heavens to attach itself to this star.

Breathe in and out of this cord, feeling the connection to this cosmic, starlight energy.

Bring this energy down into your heart.

Feel how the Earth connection joins up from your feet to meet the cosmic energy in your heart.

These energies fuse in your heart and run down your arms and out of your hands.

Feel the energy between your palms as in the previous exercise. How does it feel?

> Is there a difference in sensation? A difference in intensity? Can you pull your hands apart wide and still feel it? Enjoy the sensation.

Feel if there is somewhere in your body that wants this energy and place your hands there.

Does it want your hands to make physical contact or to be a few inches above the area?

Take as long as you need. You may want to give a few areas your attention.

When you are ready, see/feel that the roots in the Earth and the cord in the heavens are being drawn back into your body.

Take a moment to make sure that you have drawn all of your energies back to you.

When you are ready, come back and open your eyes.

How do you feel?

Practise this exercise to cultivate and develop your natural healing abilities and sensitivity. Remember that we are crystal — and that by learning to work with our own innate crystalline power, we can work more effectively with other crystals.

CHAPTER 5
Crystal therapy

Colour therapy is a powerful factor in crystal healing. People can be like magpies and are captivated by the different colours and shiny surfaces of the vast choice of stones that are available. See below a range of crystals with their known properties, but be open to your own perceptions and connections to the stones. This is just a guide.

Black

Black crystals are associated with protection, grounding and purification from negative and stagnant energy. Black is a colour of power: it contains all the other colours and is a strong absorber of energy, so if you lack energy — i.e. are experiencing depression or fatigue — use these crystals sparingly, with the exception of black tourmaline.

Black is the colour of night, the unconscious and the Shadow.

Because of their strong absorption, make sure you clear and cleanse these crystals regularly!

BLACK TOURMALINE (SCHORL)

This stone protects against geopathic and electromagnetic stress, and all types of physical pain, including spinal pain and arthritis. It balances the brain and can aid in creating new neural pathway patterns. It boosts immunity and blood circulation. Drawing out toxins from the body, it can be placed under the feet to draw them into the Earth. It can also assist with weight loss.

Black tourmaline is powerfully protective against negative energies around a person, and is the only stone that will also protect a person from their own negativity. It transmutes the negative energy into positive, and provides protection for all of the chakras. It's a good aid for depression and anxiety. This is a brilliantly useful stone that is also reasonably priced.

SHUNGITE

Shungite is best known for its purifying effect on water. It also has a detoxifying effect on the body, being antioxidant, antibacterial and antiviral. When infused into water, the liquid can be used directly on the skin for skin conditions.

Shungite shields against electromagnetic stress. It boosts the immune system and the body's vitality and is a great all-round healer of the body's internal systems and organs.

The stone is a psychic protector and absorber of negative energy. It is ideal for anyone wanting to purify themselves and their surroundings. It is grounding and can also be used to alleviate insomnia.

ONYX

Onyx is known to relieve any type of pain on the body and any type of ailment. Place it on top of the area to be treated. You can try gently rubbing it over the area to have more effect.

Onyx is great for releasing negativity from the mind, especially in the case of people finding it difficult to have a vision for the future. They may be fixated on the past or are struggling to recover from a trauma. Onyx can aid with this sort of situation. A strong psychic protector, it is grounding and boosts self-confidence.

NUUMMITE

Nuummite can have a powerful healing effect on the limbic brain and can assist with degenerative disorders. It can help with any nerve diseases, as well as the kidneys and ears. It can balance insulin production and can fight infection. A good detoxifier and pain reliever.

Known as the Sorcerer's stone, nuummite is one of the oldest minerals in the world, at three billion years old. It powerfully assists and strengthens all magical flight and journeying, intuition and clairvoyant abilities.

It can relieve insomnia and offer spiritual protection during the sleeping and waking states. It removes black magic and aids healing and liberation from old karmic patterns and entanglements.

Strengthening the auric field, it is an excellent shield against negative and unwelcome energies.

OBSIDIAN

This stone strengthens the immune system. Relieving viral and bacterial inflammation, it aids digestion and detoxification. It can lessen cramps, arthritic and joint pain.

Like all black stones, it offers protection of the energy field and grounding. It is great for shadow work — in other words, facing parts of ourselves that we do not want to see or consider undesirable. Obsidian comes from volcanic lava, so we can see how it draws out what is deeply buried. This can be challenging but can ultimately lead to greater inner peace and coming into our power without ego.

Obsidian is also a dreaming stone. It can help us to delve deeper into our unconscious, connect with our ancestors and have prophetic dreams.

Brown

Being the colour of the Earth, brown stones are grounding, comforting, calming and great for practical matters, abundance and when a sense of stability is needed. They are great for developing physical stamina, mental focus and processing strong emotions such as grief.

TIGER'S EYE

Tiger's eye can heal the eyes and enhance night vision, being able to see in the dark. It has been used to promote fertility and heal reproductive disorders, to heal broken bones and to regulate the adrenal gland and alleviate asthma.

This stone instils a sense of balanced power, encouraging a sense of drive and focus. It helps draw in your energies where they may have become distracted, scattered or lethargic. It is used to attract abundance and develop a sense for the right action to enable this.

It is also used for the cultivation of Kundalini (Divine Feminine energy) and sexual energy. It is grounding and its metallic sheen deflects negative energy.

SHIVA LINGAM

This special stone can be found in only one location: the Narmada River, one of the seven sacred rivers in India. It is a symbol of Shiva.

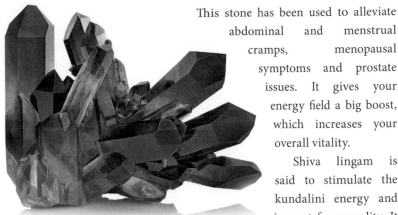

This stone has been used to alleviate abdominal and menstrual cramps, menopausal symptoms and prostate issues. It gives your energy field a big boost, which increases your overall vitality.

Shiva lingam is said to stimulate the kundalini energy and is great for sexuality. It helps remove sexual trauma, sexual energy from previous partners and shame. It contains within it the imprint of the perfect union between the Divine Masculine and Divine Feminine. It's great for couples, especially those trying for a child.

The stone connects us within our unique divine nature, enabling us to feel our interconnectedness with everyone and to recognize their divinity.

It acts as a catalyst for us to go through a process of transformation.

PIETERSITE

This stone boosts physical strength and energy. It stimulates the nervous system and the brain.

It is good for the heart and blood pressure, balancing the hormones and stimulating the pituitary gland. It is used for healing eye infections and eyesight and can ease light-headedness, headaches and difficulties in breathing.

It is also known as the Tempest stone, because if you look closely into a stone you will see a stormy swirling sky. This stone is said be a great catalyst for a strong release of pent-up emotions. If you want a more gentle and peaceful healing process, this may not be for you! Otherwise, it can really clear away stagnant energies.

The stone can help depression, especially where there is no obvious reason, bringing the motivation to succeed and create in life. It is used for addiction because it helps people to see honestly the root causes of the addiction and gives them the willpower to heal and release themselves.

SMOKY QUARTZ

The darkness of this stone varies. It is a great detoxifier, balancing the fluids in the body and encouraging the digestive system. It protects against electromagnetic frequencies and can help alleviate the effects of radiation. It is also helpful for back and shoulder pain, and strengthening the nerves.

This stone is grounding and it connects us to the divinity and beauty in the simple, mundane and everyday. It can help navigate us out of dark places, dispelling fear and depression, and bringing us into a lighter, brighter state of mind. It is calming while at the same time enabling us to take on more and to be more productive, prioritizing what is important.

Red

Red stones are energizing and motivating. They can instil you with a sense of passion and encourage you to be bolder and more assertive. Red is associated with romance and sexuality and can increase your sexual magnetism.

As the colour of blood, red is great for boosting heat, circulation, metabolism and vitality.

RED JASPER

Red jasper detoxifies and strengthens the blood and stimulates its circulation. Its strong connection to blood is evident: the Egyptians viewed it as the blood of Isis and Native Americans as the blood of Mother Earth. It has a high content of iron. It has been used to help blood-related conditions like gout and anaemia. It encourages fertility. It gives stamina and endurance but also reminds you when you need to rest.

This stone is known as a strong, nurturing stone. It gives strength and the courage to face tough challenges yet also offers a gentle, slow healing process. It brings comfort through difficult times and dealing with strong emotions. It also offers psychic protection, and protection against electromagnetic stress.

GARNET

Garnet purifies the blood and supports the heart and lungs. It detoxifies the body. It boosts the metabolism and the assimilation of minerals. It is anti-inflammatory and can aid digestion.

Garnet provides a powerful sense of purpose and strongly awakens any latent creativity to be fulfilled and carried out with passion. This red stone has the advantage of not only revitalizing the root chakra but also connecting to the heart. This boosts your life activities and relationships to a higher level of love, connection and commitment.

The stone is associated with sexuality and romance.

RUBY

Ruby is great for the heart and blood. It is beneficial for regulating the menstrual cycle and for cramps. It can help fevers and infection. It's great for circulation and vitality and can bring circulation to the lower legs and feet. This is a stone for boosting sexuality that can assist with sexual dysfunction and infertility.

Ruby gives you the courage to face life's challenges and take decisive action from a heart-centred place. It's a great stone if you are depressed or apathetic about life. It will magnify your unpleasant feelings to help you move into a more desirable state and life. This stone can feel quite intense for some people. Garnet provides a gentler alternative in this case.

In love, it is said to encourage faithful and passionate relationships. It stimulates the pineal gland and encourages good dreams.

RED ZIRCON

This stone is useful for treating spinal nerve pain and sciatica. It is said to help with schizophrenia. It can help with irregular menstrual cycles and insomnia, and can support the muscles, bones and liver. Use with caution if you have a pacemaker because it can cause dizziness.

Zircon is said to remove the energies of discrimination, and works at a genetic level. It is strongly connected with personal and collective evolution. It enables us to shed what is outgrown and no longer needed so that a new future and life and brought into manifestation. This stone is great to give the final push to someone wanting to break through to the next stage of their life and to anyone that has lost heart and vision.

It offers protection by highlighting when situations are harmful or stressful and it is time to remove ourselves from it.

Pink

Pink gemstones give out a vibration of love, kindness, gentleness, romance and happiness. They can help us develop greater empathy.

Pink is connected with the heart and can help with high blood pressure and high cholesterol.

ROSE QUARTZ

Rose quartz regulates the heartbeat. It heals and rejuvenates the sexual organs and infertility. It is healing for the brain and can help to create new neural pathways.

This is a stone for forgiveness and healing a broken heart. It helps you to develop compassion for yourself and others and to let go of anger, bitterness, disappointment and sadness. It is used to improve relationships and attract a soulmate.

KUNZITE

Kunzite stone is sometimes known as the Women's Stone because it has particular benefits for women, such as supporting the reproductive system, alleviating PMS and menstrual symptoms and supporting female puberty. It can help sciatic neuralgia, neuralgia and toothache. It is a tonic for the circulatory system and the heart. It can help to neutralize the effects of anaesthesia.

It is helpful in situations where mental and emotional balance has been severely compromised. It is said to help with mental health issues and depression. Where a person has been subjected to intense situations and heavy energies, it can remove and cleanse these influences from the energy field and then be worn or carried to create a protective field to prevent them coming back in.

It instils a deep sense of peace and creates a space where unconditional love and can be given and received. (It is not suitable for use with water.)

RHODONITE

A tonic for the lungs, this stone can alleviate emphysema. It can relieve arthritic pain, autoimmune disease and stomach ulcers. It can strengthen the muscles, circulation and encourage bone growth.

This stone is great for recovering from heartbreak and learning to forgive and release yourself from anger, resentment and even a desire for vengeance, especially if you've held onto it for a long time. This frees yourself to move into compassion towards yourself and others. The black markings in the stone create a unique quality, activating this heart but also grounding us, because the black absorbs the negativity. The stone helps us to be more patient and discerning, and less reactive. (It is not suitable for use with water.)

RHODOCHROSITE

This can alleviate irritable bowel syndrome, thyroid imbalance, migraines and abdominal pains and internal infections.

A very uplifting crystal, it promotes cheerfulness and enhances sexuality. It can heal deep-seated wounds around sexuality, abuse and anything that we need to examine and let go of. It also encourages self-love and can aid in attracting romantic love. This self-healing process then empowers us to be there actively for others and to discover our life purpose and passions and then follow through. (It is not suitable for use with water.)

MORGANITE

This stone is wonderful for the lungs and breathing, easing conditions such as emphysema and asthma. It can also help to restructure and reorganize cells.

Like all pink stones, it is a powerful emotional healer and can help us to shed anything that compromises our inner peace. Morganite has a special healing quality that can help release the fear of the unknown, enabling people to step out of familiar pain that keeps them trapped in their suffering, and encouraging them to step through that barrier.

Morganite helps us to evolve more rapidly. It also imparts upon us the ethos of equality in relationships so there is no longer a sense of superior/inferior, dominant/submissive, etc.

Orange

Orange is associated with energy, vitality, endurance, creativity and sexuality. If you want to achieve or attain something and you need a boost to keep you going in the process, then orange stones are particularly useful, especially if the process is potentially a long one.

CARNELIAN

Carnelian is good for the blood, circulation and metabolism. It boosts the lungs, heart and the digestive system. A regulator of the kidneys, it can treat lower back problems.

Carnelian is great for dispelling depression and any gloominess, laziness, tiredness and boredom.

It is said to be great for healing from abuse, and for instilling a sense of power and confidence in your own perceptions. It brings the energy and drive to complete projects with a focused and realistic vision. It is also said to be great for manifesting abundance and even making wishes come true that seemed against the odds.

Carnelian enhances our sexuality and our creative drives, giving us the incentive to express ourselves more fully.

FIRE OPAL

Fire opal can accelerate red blood cell production in the bone marrow. It can also increase immunity. It can alleviate chronic pain and relieve lower back pain.

The fire inherent in this stone helps to keep us to stay connected with the fire and passion that we have within ourselves and is particularly useful during times when we are depressed or exhausted and life has weighed us down. It reminds us of that joy, passion and excitement when we most need it.

Fire opal helps us to remain open to creative and spiritual avenues where we may have become fearful and dispirited. Fire opal is often seen as a love stone, helping to keep the fires of passion alive between a couple. (It is not suitable for use with water.)

ORANGE CALCITE

This stone is good for the digestive system and the connective tissues and skin and bones. It also improves mental clarity and memory.

Orange calcite cleanses the auric field of negative emotions and energies. It encourages discovery of new ways of living and of doing things, bringing a refreshing and progressive outlook, and the ability to leave behind what is outdated and stagnant. It instils a sense of confidence and optimism.

(It is not suitable for use with water.)

ORANGE KYANITE

Orange kyanite can help alleviate PMS, digestive problems, lower back pains, urine infections and problems in the throat and brain, as well as with blood pressure and fertility.

A powerfully high vibrational stone, it can get to the deeper roots of problems, and has the potential to release us from the karma of past life. This crystal has the capacity to invigorate and uplift all of the chakras. It boosts self-esteem and the powers of manifestation. It can help free us from any links we have to previous sexual partners that are a drain on our energy. (It is not suitable for use with water.)

Yellow/Gold

These stones are fantastic for bringing positivity, zest and energy into your life. They are great for manifestation and attracting abundance. Yellow or gold stones strengthen your sense of personal power, confidence and assertiveness. They are wonderful for strengthening communication on a personal level or within a group or family setting.

CITRINE

This stone can balance the digestive system, and energize the spleen and pancreas. It can regenerate tissues, alleviate kidney and bladder infections, boost the immune system and lessen symptoms of chronic fatigue.

Citrine is protective because of its highly positive energy. It transmutes negativity from your own thoughts and emotions, or from the energies around you, into positivity. It is one of the only stones that does not need cleansing. This stone can be used for releasing physical and emotional trauma.

It is also well-known for being an attractor of abundance. This is not purely by luck but by tapping us into our own resources and potential so we can see what we need to do and have the energy and confidence to follow through. It also clears the mindset of lack that prevents us from manifesting.

It is great for interpersonal communication and can be placed in a room where discussions are had to ensure they go more smoothly. In terms of romance, citrine crystals improve communication between couples and can be brilliant for attracting a partner because they increase your confidence and magnetism. Citrine's protective qualities can help to ward off people who could be a negative influence on you and enable you to be more discerning.

AMBER

Amber is not actually a crystal, it is a resin. Even so, it is widely used by crystal healers. It comes in shades of brown, orange, red and green. It is good for the stomach, spleen, pancreas, gallbladder, liver, joints, glands and intestines. It can be placed over any of these or over any wounds to promote healing. To balance your whole system, place over the thymus gland an inch below the dip between your collar bones.

This stone protects against negative energies from others and the environment, enabling people to set healthy boundaries. It is uplifting and helps those who are depressed and feel stuck in life to empower them to see a way forward and fresh options. It is a light in the darkness. Amber can cleanse all of the chakras. (It is not suitable for use with water.)

GOLDEN TOPAZ

This stone aids digestion, nerve problems, eating disorders and the metabolism, as well as female fertility.

Topaz is said to receive its power from the Sun. Golden topaz gives a powerful boost to our self-confidence and a sense of pride to our individuality.

It is a strong stone to assist us with manifestation, especially for people who seem to struggle with this. It will help them to understand where they sabotage themselves so that they can begin to manifest what they want effectively. It can also increase the sense

of synchronicity that is necessary for manifestation. Golden topaz brings peace to people and is energizing.

YELLOW APATITE

Yellow apatite can aid detoxification, speed up the metabolism and address issues around appetite and weight loss. It is great for strengthening bones, joints and cartilage. It is said to improve posture, reduce wrinkles and assist in breaking down a build-up of excess fluorite in the pineal gland.

Yellow apatite is highly stimulating to the mind and can boost creativity and inventiveness. It can also increase third eye visions, psychic perceptions and communication with the spirit world.

It increases personal power and can embolden you to try new things and push yourself out of your comfort zone to manifest your dreams. It can also assist shyness in social situations, improving communication and understanding the needs of others. (It is not suitable for prolonged contact with water.)

Green

Green is the colour of nature and these stones soothe us, calm us down and offer rejuvenation in a calm way. Green is also associated with luck and prosperity. It is one of the colours of the Heart chakra and encourages positive relationships based on kindness and compassion.

MOSS AGATE

This stone is said to help with childbirth, relieving the pain and easing the process. It helps the body recover after illness, and can bring relief to coughs, colds and fever.

It stimulates the brain, helping with concentration and analytical abilities. It can also help with processing and organizing information.

Moss agate can help us to become more understanding within our relationships. It brings emotional balance by enabling us to understand our emotions without being ruled by them.

It has a strong connection to nature, and plants can benefit from having a piece placed next to them.

AVENTURINE

This stone is said to lower cholesterol, as well as balance the thymus gland and blood pressure. It can prevent heart attacks and reduce inflammation in the body.

Aventurine is strongly associated with the healing of any trauma, social or familial conditioning that we experienced from the time of birth to the age of seven, and which is now holding us back. Working with aventurine can clear these blocks and wounds, enabling a powerful process of liberation and transformation to occur.

It is known as a Stone of Adventures, making us more open to new ideas and other peoples' suggestions; the impossible seems to become possible. It is said to be protective for travellers, and also shields against electro-magnetic smog.

EMERALD

Emerald is a great tonic for all of the organs, but it has particular affinity with the heart, both physically and energetically. It also detoxifies the liver. It can soothe eye infections and improve eyesight.

Emerald is known for a being a stone to attract a happy and harmonious love relationship that lasts the test of time. It brings us into a state of unconditional love and emotional peace.

It also exposes situations where dishonesty and deceit are at play. Enhancing our own sense of discernment, it gives us a clear perception of the realities around us.

Emerald enhances psychic vision and increases prophetic abilities. The stone also attracts abundance.

MALACHITE

Malachite has a reputation for easing all sorts of female problems like menstrual cramps and childbirth. It also eases sexual discomfort, especially when caused by trauma. It stimulates the nerves, brain and liver, and can help those suffering from arthritis. It is a very protective stone against negative energies, as well as electromagnetic and environmental stress.

Malachite is a strongly transformative stone. Some people may find its energy a little too intense. But if you are willing to be challenged, it will show you where you need to change to free and heal yourself from where you are sabotaging yourself. It can clear trauma and karmic patterns.

It is an empowering stone, giving you the courage to be yourself and to be seen as visible in the world, while at the same time having empathy and openness for others. (It is not suitable for use with water.)

NEPHRITE

This stone is great for overall health and vitality. It is known as a kidney and bladder healer; a detoxifier. It boosts the immune system and enhances fertility.

It brings about emotional balance and serenity, as it is soothing and grounding to a troubled or overactive mind. It gives you the calm determination to create a happy life for yourself.

Nephrite is great for dreaming and having good-quality sleep. It can improve dream recall and the ability to lucid dream.

Neprite is an auspicious stone to attract abundance and success.

Blue

B lue stones are cooling and calming. Blue also has a strong connection with the throat chakra and communication. Blue stimulates the intuition and the imagination, yet also helps rational thinking because it cools down the emotions.

Physically, it cools down heat-related conditions.

AQUAMARINE

Aquamarine is great for the eyes. It balances the pituitary and thyroid gland, eases allergy and hay fever symptoms, and strengthens the teeth and gums.

It is a wonderful stone for calming and focusing the mind so that you can resolve problems with clarity and simplicity. Great for dealing with conflict, aquamarine brings compassion, understanding and the ability to communicate about challenging matters with a cool head. It also brings hope. It is a type of 'truth serum' stone, so if you have difficulty speaking your mind, carry or wear a piece of this stone.

Aquamarine is useful stone for writers and speakers.

It has associations with the sea, mermaids and the deities of the sea. It is used as a protection talisman for travel, particularly across oceans.

It is a stone of spiritual vision and has been used for scrying and predicting the future.

LABRADORITE

Labradorite is said to harmonize blood pressure and metabolism. It also increases tolerance to cold and can alleviate inflammatory conditions such as gout and rheumatism.

Inuit tradition claims that this stone was not of Earthly origin and that it fell from the frozen fire of the Aurora Borealis. Known as a Stone of Magic, this is a great stone for psychic readers because it enables you to read the energy of other people, places and situation without taking those energies on. It's a strong protector, keeping you within the realms of your own energetic boundaries.

Labradorite keeps the thought processes focused and unified, and can bring up forgotten memories. It is great for understanding the truth behind situations in our lives, and can dispel illusions.

BLUE LACE AGATE

Blue lace agate is good for cooling down any condition that involves an excess of heat in the body such as fever, inflammation and arthritis. It can balance the fluids in the brain.

Equally it is useful on a mental/emotional level, where someone is hot-headed in temperament or there is a situation where communication is needed and emotions are flying high. Blue lace agate can stop people from being reactive and lashing out verbally and find a way to communicate from a place of wisdom. It teaches us to open our hearts, even in charged situations, lessening the effects of destructive communication. It helps people express their thoughts and feelings more freely.

LAPIS LAZULI

Lapis lazuli is balancing for the pituitary and thyroid gland and the whole of the endocrine system. It helps with problems in the throat, larynx and vocal cords.

This is a stone of profound truth. It facilitates expression and speaking the truth. It also puts you in touch with your true purpose and how you really feel about things deep inside you. This can lead to a process of shedding what no longer serves you and what is not authentic in your life so that you can be reborn into a new way of being.

It's a stone of friendship and is beneficial for improving relationships. It has had strong associations with royalty and can be useful if you want to achieve fame or public recognition within your field. (It is not suitable for prolonged contact with water.)

LARIMAR

This stone can alleviate any excessive heat-related conditions like inflammation, infections, ulcers and sunburn. It can clear all the meridians and heal problems in the head, throat and chest.

Larimar cools heated and excessive emotion like anger, fear, resentment and anguish. It releases the emotions and brings calm, opening us to wider perspectives. A communication stone, it enables us to express our feelings and needs, openly and gently.

Larimar connects us with the Divine Feminine but also with a sense of childlikeness and creativity so that we can move freely with the flow of life.

It is linked with the Sea and is also said to assist soulmates coming together. (It is not suitable for prolonged contact with water.)

Purple

Purple stones calm an overactive and anxious mind. They improve sleep and can help activate dream activity, as they also stimulate the pineal gland. This can also increase spiritual visions and insights, especially during meditation.

Purple stones are magical, tapping us into our creativity and imagination, which we can use to change and create our outer world.

AMETHYST

Amethyst is good for relieving headaches, migraines and insomnia. It boosts the production of hormones and can ease tinnitus.

It is a stone of wisdom and spiritual insight. It brings a down-to-earth spirituality, connecting to higher wisdom but in a tempered way, helping us to keep a level head. It is a stone that both grounds and revitalizes us. It brings a sense of peace while remaining alert. For people who have lost their way, amethyst can bring them back onto their path with calm purpose.

It has a legendary reputation for helping to retain a state of sobriety when drinking, especially when drinking out of an amethyst cup.

CHAROITE

Charoite is a tonic for the eyes, liver and pancreas. It is a pain reliever, soothing the nerves and easing cramps. It is good for insomnia too.

Charoite gives support and comfort to people who are isolated and living in adverse circumstances. It gives endurance.

It has the quality of assisting people to step into their absolute individuality and gifts without compromise. It gives people the courage to live those things, even if there is strong pressure and expectations from those around them. Chaorite is a liberating and emboldening force.

A great help to mental health, it releases deep fears, extreme negativity and obsessional thoughts, and allows for a more relaxed and positive outlook. (It is not suitable for prolonged contact with water.)

LEPIDOLITE

This stone helps to alleviate joint and nerve pain, sciatica and neuralgia. It is great for insomnia and also healing for the skin.

Lepidolite contains lithium, which is an important ingredient in anxiety medicine. It follows that this is an excellent stone for anxiety, and is best when worn with direct contact on the skin. It facilitates deep emotional healing.

This stone puts you in touch with your mind and heart in a way that they can work in harmony with each other. It enables you to keep a focused and rational mind while listening to your heart. It helps you shed outdated patterns to move forward into the future.

A magical stone that aids astral and shamanic travel, it is said to have a strong connection with the fairy folk. (It is not suitable for contact with water.)

IOLITE

Iolite is a strong detoxifier of the liver and the whole body, decreasing fatty deposits and preventing the build-up of cholesterol. It strengthens the auric field and stimulates the pituitary gland. It contains iron and magnesium.

It is a powerful stone for inner and psychic vision and for developing these abilities. It is also useful for tuning into your life vision and revealing deeper insights.

This stone brings on an independent attitude, particularly useful if you are in a co-dependent relationship. (It is not suitable for prolonged contact with water.)

White

White is the colour of the Moon, purity, innocence and femininity. White is a great colour for cleansing, bringing serenity, peace and calm.

White stones cast light into the dark. They are said to be easy to programme with intentions.

SELENITE

Selenite is great for the bones, particularly the spine, realigning it and increasing flexibility. It is a tonic for the prostate.

It is very soothing and clearing for the mind, releasing pent-up emotions that may be the cause of illnesses. It purifies the auric field from denser, heavier energies.

Selenite has a strong link to angels and is a form of divine light. It is great for creating a stronger spiritual connection and insight.

(It is not suitable for contact with water.)

PETALITE

Petalite has been used as a pain reliever. It is also a tonic for the heart, nerves and eyes. It can give psychic guidance into the root cause of illnesses.

This stone works at healing and releases karmic and ancestral causes of problems. It also releases negative cords between people, freeing you to move into a happier future, shedding old detrimental patterns and baggage.

It contains lithium and can be used to ease depression.

This stone is connected with the angelic realms and is a great stone to increase your connection to spiritual awareness.

PEARL

Pearl, while not a crystal, is wonderful for women. It balances hormones, regulating the menstrual cycle and easing the process of childbirth. It also balances the fluids in the body and is beneficial for the eyes, ears, teeth and jaw.

Pearl is an ultra-feminine gem, bringing peace and purity of the body and energy field. It allows us to be in touch with our emotions, reaching to a new depth. Pearl goes through an intense process of creation, reminding us of the importance of our own processes so we can accept them more.

It connects us to the more spiritual aspects of sexuality, and so is a good gemstone for relationships.

(It is not suitable for use with water.)

HOWLITE

Howlite is good for the bones because it has a balancing effect on how calcium is distributed in the body. It strengthens bones, teeth and soft tissues, and so can alleviate conditions such as osteoporosis. It is also helpful for nausea and can lessen vomiting.

Howlite is a soothing crystal, which can absorb nervous tension and relieve anxiety. It aids peaceful sleep and is a lucid dreaming crystal. It is a gentle and nurturing stone that teaches us patience, calming anger and intense emotions.

The thin black lines give howlite a grounding and focused quality, which allows us to reach spiritual heights without losing our connection to physical reality.

Howlite is a great stone for seeing creative possibilities and potential rather than seeing obstacles everywhere. (It is not suitable for use with water.)

MOONSTONE

This stone balances hormones and aligns them to the cycles of nature. It helps with menstrual issues, childbirth and menopause, and increases fertility. It is a stone linked to longevity and lessens fluid retention.

Traditionally known as a traveller's stone, it is said to offer protection while travelling, particularly over water. Also known as a stone for lovers, it is a traditional wedding gift and is reputed to bring passion and fertility.

Moonstone is soothing to the emotions and assists us to delve deeper into our own emotions, releasing those that do not serve us and giving us a greater understanding of our inner nature.

It opens up the Crown chakra, connecting us to divine inspiration. It helps us tap into our dreams, wishes and a sense of magic and synchronicity to attract things to us. Obviously, it strengthens our connection to the Moon and its cycles. A dreaming stone, it helps us to release tension and receive pleasant dreams.

Clear

Clear crystals have a magnifying effect. They are the easiest to programme, being the fastest and most effective to manifest. Use them wisely, with pure intentions, to create the most positive results for yourself.

They are great for clarifying the mind and matters in your life, and for relieving fatigue. They greatly expand consciousness and are great for meditation and spiritual journeying.

CLEAR QUARTZ

Clear quartz is the best known crystal and is often the stone that people first associate with crystals. It stimulates the blood and immune system, making it a great tonic for the body against any illnesses. It strengthens the heart and nervous system, cleans out the urinary system and kidneys, and regenerates cells.

Clear quartz purifies and amplifies all of the chakras and the auric field. It is a stone of expansion and evolution. It encourages you to grow into your full potential, to see and realize your dreams. It can also reveal to you where your actions and thoughts are leading you. If this is undesirable, the information can empower you to change your course. It is a master crystal.

Clear quartz gives you absolute clarity. It is fantastic for manifestation, attuning itself to your frequency and giving you what you need.

APOPHYLLITE

Apophyllite can alleviate asthma, especially when caused by allergies, and is a tonic for the lungs and the respiratory system. It has a high water content, so by energetic osmosis can assist the rehydration of eyes and mucous membranes. It is healing for eye problems.

This stone facilitates dreaming and astral travel. It stimulates the pineal gland, opening the third eye and clairvoyant abilities.

Apophyllite quells anxiety and helps you become outgoing, expressing who you are and being honest. It also gives clarity about your choices and where they are taking you, so you can review your actions and decisions. (It is not suitable for prolonged use in water.)

HERKIMER DIAMOND

This stone is good for the nerves and the brain, assisting in creating new neural pathways. It boosts metabolism, detoxification and cellular structure.

It is extremely effective for stress relief and is considered very powerful in dealing with the specific stress that leads to cancer growing in the body. It can release this and the memories associated with it.

Herkimer diamond is the hardest type of quartz available and contains even more light, making it a very high vibrational stone. It shows you a much higher perspective and attunes you to the highest potential of your soul. Herkimer diamond has the power to transform and offer profound healing. It facilitates the process of

coming completely into yourself so that you can allow life to happen around you, rather than striving to create and control.

It helps dream recall, telepathy and spiritual vision. It can cleanse and revitalize all of the chakras.

This stone is more suited to sleeping or meditating with, rather than wearing as jewellery.

CLEAR CALCITE

Clear calcite detoxifies the body. It is good for the kidneys and the eyes. It is a tonic for the mucous membranes, skin, teeth and connective tissues.

A fantastic stone for the mind, it assists with heightening the IQ, focusing the mind where it may be fragmented. It also promotes quicker thinking, learning, memory and confidence.

Clear calcite purifies all of the chakras and releases stress, so it can bring on a state of peace and calm.

It encourages you to embrace the new and try new experiences and ways of doing things. It is energizing and motivating. (It is not suitable for use with water.)

Multicoloured

Multicoloured stones vary in healing properties because each has a different and unique combination of colours. They represent versatility, diversity and creativity.

WATERMELON TOURMALINE

Watermelon tourmaline is strengthening for the heart. It regenerates nerves and muscles. It calms stomach upset.

The stone is a powerful heart healer: green and pink both being heart chakra colours. It can facilitate deep heart healing, going into any trauma and lingering emotional hurt that needs to be cleansed and released. This leaves the person much more open to trust and take joy in life, becoming freer to give love to whoever they come into contact with and strengthening all inter-personal relationships.

A great stone for healing depression and anxiety, giving a brighter and more playful outlook on life.

RAINBOW FLUORITE

Fluorite strengthens the bones and teeth. As an anti-inflammatory, it can relieve arthritis and soothe painful muscles. It is good for colds and flu.

Fluorite is great for the mind, increasing intelligence, bringing organization and focus to thought processes. All the colours in rainbow fluorite enable us to see things from many perspectives and have an open mind. It helps discernment while at the same time not taking a judgemental attitude to help make clearer decisions.

It is great for communication and creative thinking. It increases positivity while enabling us to trust more in our intuition.

It protects against and clears from electromagnetic frequencies. (It is not suitable for use with water.)

BLOODSTONE

This stone fortifies the blood, heart and circulation. It is considered to be a strong detoxifier.

It detoxifies on every level, purifying the energy field. Its connection to the blood gives healing to your bloodline. When you start to use this stone, you need to allow a process of physical and energetic detoxification because it will be bringing in fresh energy and a fresh way of living.

This stone is revitalizing and brings you courage. It also helps you to stay in your truth and honour. (It is not suitable for prolonged contact with water.)

OPAL

Opal has a high water content and is good for the lymph and the blood. It is also high in silica and strengthens the hair, nails and skin.

Due to its water association, opal helps us work with our emotions. It magnifies whatever we are feeling, our desires and how that is making our life play out. That can be a pleasurable experience, and if it isn't, we can look at how to change this. It is also used for spiritual vision and journeying. It brings a sense of joy, calm and security. It is also protective. (It is not suitable for use with water.)

AMETRINE

This stone is a combination of amethyst and citrine. It can help with detoxification, circulation, skin problems, allergies, migraines and joint pain.

It is useful for insomnia. The amethyst part soothes the nervous system, making sleep easier, while the citrine part energizes, giving you the energy to perform during the waking hours.

It is a great combination of masculine and feminine energies. This enables you to have a connection to the spiritual world and carry out your practical tasks and keep focus. The stone helps to enhance the powers of manifestation.

Ametrine is helpful for overcoming addictions and losing weight. It also helps you to recognize your destructive habits so you can shed them.

It is great for personal relations and friendships, helping you to improve a sense of connection with everyone, including those you might consider difficult or even enemies. It is a great transmuter of negative energies.

Ametrine can be used to help you attract or call in your soul tribe. This a group of people that have a particular affinity with you on a soul level.

Metallic

Metallic stones magnify the energy field of the wearer and other stones that are worn with them.

PYRITE

This can relieve joint pain and back pain and is also good for cramps, including menstrual. It can help with fevers and the digestive system.

This stone offers strong protection to the auric field, magnifying it and making it larger. It also gives greater courage to put in place your own boundaries. It is revitalizing and is great for the mind, giving focus, purpose and greater memory.

It gives a stronger sense of self-esteem and confidence in your own abilities.

Pyrite activates our Soul Star chakra, which connects us to our higher self. (It is not suitable for use with water.)

HEMATITE

Hematite is good for the blood and the circulatory system. It also helps to remove excess heat from the body, so is useful for conditions such as arthritis and chronic inflammation.

It is an extremely grounding stone, allowing you to make clearer more discerning decisions and calming down intense emotions. This grounding effect makes hematite a useful stone for easing the effects of shock. It activates the Earth Star chakra. If you are a person who tends to take spiritual flight regularly and are ungrounded, this is an excellent stone to counteract that tendency.

Hematite is very protective, shielding your energy field. It brings courage and optimism. It lessens the effects of electromagnetic smog. (It is not suitable for use with water.)

COPPER

Another substance that isn't a crystal, but has strong healing powers. Many people wear copper bracelets to relieve arthritis, rheumatism and other issues stemming from inflammation, as it detoxifies the joints. Copper also boosts blood circulation and revitalizes the heart.

Copper is said to contain the energies of both the sun and the moon. Traditionally it is associated with Venus, giving it a reputation as a love stone. It helps to attract love and address any sexual issues.

It is reputed to be great for attracting abundance. It is also an energy amplifier and conductor. It can enhance psychic abilities.

Copper is an absorber of negative energies, so when it becomes dull you know it is time to cleanse it. You can do this using warm water, lemon and salt. Copper tarnishes, so it needs to be cleaned from time to time.

CHAPTER 6
Different crystal shapes

Not only do the different types of crystals have their own properties, but the actual shape of the stone itself—whether natural or man-made—has a bearing on what the stone can be used for. Here we look at a number of shapes that crystals come in and how that affects how they are used in healing.

Single terminator crystal

These crystals, often quartz or different varieties of quartz, have a wand-like shape with one side ending in a singular point that sends direct energy towards whichever direction it is pointing. You can direct energy around the body in a particular way —for instance, down the legs and out of the feet, to be grounded. Or you can direct more energy into another stone or out of a stone. This point can also be used literally like a wand to activate energies in stones by tracing circles either clockwise or counter-clockwise. The point can energetically connect stones together as well.

Take 2 small single terminator crystals (preferably clear quartz) and place one in each palm. Point the one in the left palm up towards the arm and the one in the right palm down towards the fingers.

The left hand receives energy and the right hand sends out energy. Feel the flow in your hands and how it moves through your auric field. This helps us harmonize the polarities within us: masculine/feminine, giving/receiving. It is also very soothing and helps keep our auric field and mind clear. This encourages the flow of energy in our hands, which is useful if you are wanting to open up and balance your hand chakras.

Double terminator crystals

These are similar to the single terminator except they have a point at either end and look quite symmetrical. This has a balancing and equalizing effect. It is useful for discharging energy as both points are facing outwards.

Place on the third eye, angled horizontally. This balances the left and right side of the brain. Particularly good if you have a tendency to strongly emphasize one way of thinking and perceiving. For instance, if you are strongly rationalistic and cannot connect with your intuition and imagination—or vice versa.

Twin crystal (Soulmate quartz)

This crystal looks like two single terminators that have been fused together with the points facing the same direction. These are good for attracting love relationships and for harmonizing any kind of relationship.

When having difficulties in a relationship, ask this crystal to help you. Place it between you and the other person and have an honest, open and compassionate discussion about your differences.

If you are seeking a romantic partner, programme this crystal to assist you to find a compatible partner, and carry it with you as you go about your life.

Crystal cluster

This is made up of many crystal points growing out of a bed of rock—often quartz or amethyst. They are a great boost for a room to keep the energies clear and vibrant. They also inspire creativity and inventiveness, and are good for attracting abundance and for business.

Place your crystals on a cluster for 24 hours to cleanse and recharge them.

Sphere/Ball

These crystals have been deliberately made into a perfectly spherical shape. This represents unity and integrity. Balls carry a harmonious vibration that can be useful for group situations, to help people work together with ease.

Traditionally these were used for scrying, and crystal balls were associated with fortune-tellers. They can also be used for simple meditation or indeed to develop psychic vision to gain access to information and insight. Any form of crystal can be used. I recommend ones that have no markings or lines because they are easier. But go with what attracts you.

Place your crystal ball in front of you. Sit in a comfortable position where your spine is straight. This allows your energy to move more freely and to keep focus. Darkening the room can make this process easier and it relaxes the mind to be able to receive more intuition.

Gaze at the ball and soften your focus. Gaze without trying to force anything. Just allow your mind to relax, and notice if any images or feelings begin to arise in you. Trust and witness whatever comes up.

Remember, this process can require patience!

You can programme your ball before scrying to ask it to help you develop your abilities. Make sure that you clear the ball thoroughly before and after each session. There are some methods for cleansing given on pages 19-20.

Pyramid

Pyramids are an ancient sacred geometry symbol, representing the human yearning for enlightenment. They connect heaven and Earth: the square structure of the base reaching up to the apex, while the point channels energy from the cosmos down to the Earth. Equally, energy or intentions can be channelled up and out through the apex point.

Copper pyramid structures are used for meditation. They are said to greatly enhance the experience and ability to receive divine guidance and intuition while cleansing and clearing your energy body. It is said that fruit and vegetables kept inside them stay fresh for longer.

Write down an intention that you would like to see come true. Then fold up the paper and place it under a crystal pyramid to bring greater manifestation power.

Crystal skull

The skull itself is representative of consciousness. Ancient cultures, particularly the Mesoamerican, viewed them as sacred objects. Most of them were made from quartz, which was also seen as the brain cells of Mother Earth. They can have knowledge and information stored inside them. Antique skulls are said to have information that can be received clairvoyantly.

The skull also has a connection with death. We can use these skulls to communicate with our deceased ancestors. They are also here to serve the purpose of helping us to recognize where we need to change our lives. And to shed what we need to shed so that we can shift, transform and move forward with more ease.

They help us to develop our psychic abilities and expand our consciousness.

Call a deceased relative or ancestor into your skull to communicate with them. This can create healing in your bloodline. The Day of the Dead is the ideal time.

Light a candle and place it before the skull. Say their name out loud and ask them to come into the skull. If you don't know their name, just say, for example, "Great-great-grandmother, come into the skull."

Look into the skull's eyes and say their name. Tell them that they are dead and that they are loved. Say whatever you would like to say to them.

If you didn't know them, introduce yourself. Tell them about your life.

If there were problems with this person with you or within the family, you can talk about this.

Tell them you are honoured to make this connection.

When you are finished, thank them and bid them farewell.

This interaction can bring about healing and shifts.

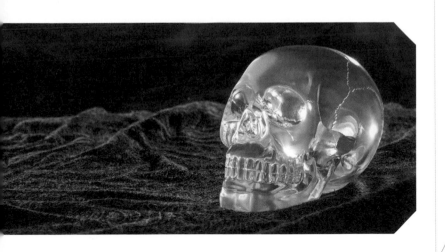

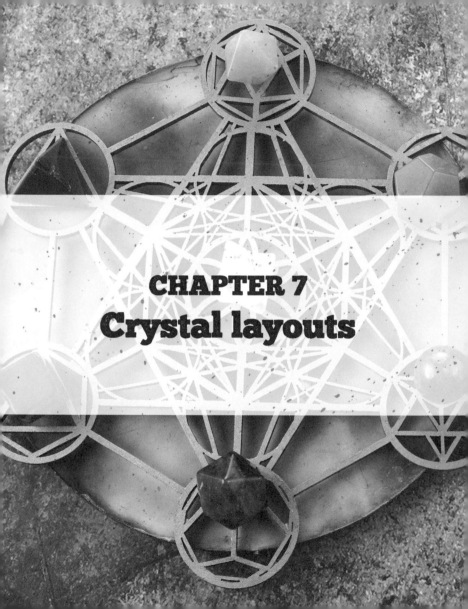

CHAPTER 7
Crystal layouts

SEVEN CHAKRA LAYOUTS WITH VARIATIONS

This can be done with 7 clear quartz tumblestones (quartz can be used on any of the chakras) or with 7 different chakra stones.

Prepare yourself to lie down and place a stone on each chakra. State your intention to the crystals that they are going to heal and balance your chakras.

If you are using the different chakra stones, you may want to place the stones up the side of your body in rough alignment with your own chakras.

Lie down and put the crystals on your chakras. Breathe, relax and feel the sensations in your chakras and how the crystals are interacting with them. Take about 15–20 minutes to immerse yourself in the experience.

Then take the crystals off your body. Have a glass of water and integrate the experience.

Earth Star and Soul Star Chakra

For added potency and a sense of greater expansion, try adding hematite on the Earth Star and pyrite on the Soul Star chakra. This will be easier if you lie down first. Map where these two chakras lie, and sit up and place the stones on these ones first. Then lie down to put on the other stones.

SINGLE TERMINATOR GRID FOR CHAKRAS THAT NEED EXTRA SUPPORT

You will need 4 small terminator quartz points. This is where your pendulum can come in handy. You can ask it which of your 7 chakras needs extra attention today. Use

the pendulum to ask for each of them until you receive a 'yes' for one. Place a crystal representing that chakra in front of you.

Ask if your chakra needs energy to be discharged or boosted. When energy needs discharging, place the pointers at the four sides of the chakra crystal, like the compass points, with the 4 points pointing away from the crystal.

When the chakra needs boosting, place the pointers towards the crystal.

CHAKRA TONING

Toning is a sound healing technique where you make vocal sounds to clear, heal and balance your energy. With chakra toning, there are specific sounds for each chakra. The chakras have specific mantras in Sanskrit and there are also vowel chants – as listed below. I learned the vowel chants via Jonathan Goldman, a well-known sound healer. Vowels are said to be more conducive to energy flow, whereas consonants break up energy flow. Personally, I find the vowels more effective, but try them both and see what your own experience is.

This is mostly done by starting at the root chakra and working your way up. But if you feel you need more grounding, start from the crown and work down to the root. The idea is that you are singing a note up or down every time you move through the chakras. I recommend toning at least 3 times at each chakra.

Start gently to allow your voice to warm up. Forcing your voice, especially at the beginning, can strain your vocal cords.

There are plenty of free videos online which you can follow if you prefer to be guided. These also help you with pitching the sounds.

Adding toning to your chakra layout has the added benefit of clearing and strengthening your throat chakra. The sound vibrations will further activate the crystals.

Chakra	Sanskrit	Vowel Sound	Crystals
Root	LAM	Uh	Red jasper and garnet
Sacral	VAM	Ooo	Carnelian
Solar plexus	RAM	Oh	Citrine and tiger's eye
Heart	YAM	Ah	Rose quartz and malachite
Throat	HAM	Eye (eye-ee)	Blue lace agate and lapis lazuli
Third eye	OM	Ey	Lapis lazuli and amethyst
Crown	OM	Eee	Amethyst and moonstone

BLACK TOURMALINE PROTECTION GRID

For this you need 5 pieces of black tourmaline. The size is not important.

Programme the stones to create a grid of protection around you.

Place them in the shape of a 5-pointed star that is big enough for you to lie in, with the apex of the star above your head. 5 is the number of the human as we have 4 limbs plus our head.

Using either your index finger or a single terminator quartz crystal, join the 5 crystals. You can do this standing up and then lying inside the grid or while lying in the grid.

Start at the top point above your head, and trace to the one below your left foot. Then up to the one by your right arm. Next, across the torso over to the one by your left arm. Then down to the one under your right foot. Finally, join back up to the top of your head.

Use this grid if you are going to be in an environment or situation where you feel an extra shield of protection would be beneficial. It tends to last for a day.

LAYOUT FOR GROUNDING

Use this layout to ground yourself. If you are anxious, stressed or your work involves a lot of intellectual ideas and information, you could benefit from grounding and strengthening your connection to the Earth. If you have problems in your knees or ankles, you can also use this to release blocked energy into the Earth.

For this you need: 2 gemstones to be placed under the feet: hematite, smoky quartz or, if you are working with knee or ankle problems, I recommend amethyst. Place 1 hematite between the feet and 2 small single terminator quartz crystals.

For this layout, sit on a chair with your feet placed firmly on the ground.

Programme the 2 crystals for your feet to strengthen your grounding to the Earth or to release any blockages from your ankles and knees into the Earth. Place the 2 crystals on the ground, under the ball of your foot and in line with the bottom of the second toe. There is a natural dip here. This is the Kidney 1 point according to shiatsu, and is a point where you can take in energies from, and release energies into, the Earth.

Take the piece of hematite and programme it to activate the Earth Star chakra below you in the Earth, then place it between your feet.

Programme the 2 single terminator crystals to assist with the release of any energies that need to be discharged into the Earth. Place one on each thigh with the terminator point facing downwards towards the knees, directing the energy flow downwards.

Sit with this for about 15 minutes. Take slow, deep breaths into your lower abdomen. Allowing your mind and your energies to settle and ground.

Visualize/feel roots growing out from the soles of your feet and growing down until they reach the core of the Earth.

Visualize/feel that these roots are taking in and releasing energy from the Earth and that this connection is strengthening more and more.

THIRD EYE LAYOUT

This layout is powerful for opening up clairvoyant abilities, recalling dreams, experiencing lucid dreams and enhancing the ability to receive wisdom from the spiritual realms.

I always recommend being grounded energetically before working with the upper chakras. If you are not grounded, you can end up with headaches, insomnia and fatigue. If you feel you would benefit from grounding, perform the above grounding layout a day or two before using this one. If you are doing this for dreaming, I recommend doing it before you go to sleep.

You will need 1 apophyllite, 1 lapis lazuli (or any third-eye crystal such as the merkaba, shown), 1 hematite and 1 pyrite crystal.

Programme the apophyllite and third-eye crystal of choice to open your dreaming or spiritual vision abilities.

Programme the hematite to activate your Earth Star chakra. This will keep you grounded and bring you back safely from whatever journeys that you go on.

Programme the pyrite to activate your Soul Star chakra. This connects you more fully to your soul and your higher self, enabling you to receive spiritual messages and information (particularly about past lives).

Lie down for this layout. Place the pyrite and hematite on your Soul Star and Earth Star chakra.

Place the apophyllite just above your head at the Crown chakra.

Place the third-eye stone at the point between your eyebrows.

Relax and enjoy the experience for 15–20

minutes. make a note of any sensations and perceptions that may arise.

If you are using this for dreaming, put the crystals next to where you are sleeping for an enhanced effect. Remember to place a journal beside your bed to record any insights you may gain in your dreams.

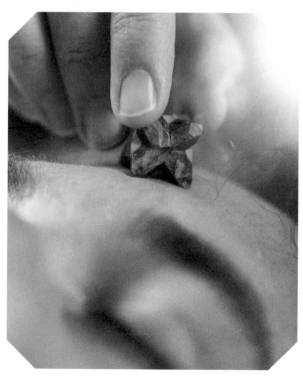

CHAPTER 8
Crystals around the home and grids

Crystals can be placed around the home to enhance the flow of energy and the harmony. We can use them to create good Feng shui. Feng shui is a Chinese system based on creating harmony, prosperity, health and good relationships by the arrangement of furniture and objects in the room with reference to the cardinal directions and the surrounding features of nature.

If you are an avid collector of crystals, just be aware that they are powerful and that having many can create an intense field energetically. This may not always be beneficial, as the energies can be incompatible with each other and your needs. It's a good idea to cleanse and charge them regularly because they absorb so many energies. If they are loaded up with stagnant energies, they could be contributing more harm than good to your environment.

Protection

Crystals are an excellent way to provide energetic protection in your home, creating that sense of sanctuary. They can protect you from the electromagnetic frequencies of your own electronic devices and your surroundings, and from negative energies, including your own, which are created by stress and arguments. If you live in a densely populated area or a block of flats, they can shield you from other people's emotions and problems.

Black tourmaline, shungite, smoky quartz and clear quartz are particularly good for this purpose. You can place a piece in each corner of your home or a particular room. With smoky quartz, you can use pointed ones. Place the points outwards to draw out the negative energies or point them in to draw in healing light and energy. Placement of these next to windows is also good.

Abundance

Citrine and tiger's eye are particularly good for attracting abundance. You can place one in each corner of the home, living room or office. They are also energizing stones full of positive energy, so great for creating a dynamic and positive atmosphere for communing, work and study.

A piece of garnet or ruby in a place where you keep money can further attract wealth.

Where to place crystals

LIVING ROOM

A citrine piece on the coffee table or somewhere central in the living room is great for creating good communication and understanding between people who live and socialize in this space. Rose quartz is also positive for creating a loving, supportive atmosphere.

Any sphere-shaped crystal is helpful for creating harmony when there is more than one person living together and bringing a sense of unity.

Selenite can be found in the form of towers, but any form is beneficial because they clear stagnant and negative energies and bring more light into a place. They also bring soothing energy.

KITCHEN

Yellow apatite, citrine and carnelian are stones that help to encourage healthy eating, so if you want to improve your diet and health, these are good stones to help you. These stones also bring out creativity, which can add flair and innovation to your cooking.

Food was traditionally put into copper pyramids to preserve its shelf life. It is said to help retain their life force for longer.

OFFICE/WORKSPACE

As mentioned before, crystals are useful for protection against electromagnetic frequencies, so place stones such as shungite, black tourmaline and smoky quartz around your electronic devices.

Citrine, fluorite and apatite are all great for stimulating and focusing the mind. Tiger's eye and garnet help you to have the determination and stamina to see through projects and tasks. Citrine, blue lace agate and aquamarine can help you communicate more skilfully with colleagues and customers.

BEDROOM

Rose quartz helps to create a loving and romantic atmosphere for relationships. If you are seeking a relationship, this stone can help you to attract that too.

Moonstone, amethyst and any purple stones can help you sleep more peacefully, especially if there are problems with insomnia. They can also bring about good dreams.

Crystal grids to place around the home

Crystal grids are a practice whereby crystals are chosen and placed in a particular arrangement called a grid. These are used as a tool of manifestation or magic to bring about a particular desire, such as healing, a relationship, a job or money.

I will suggest a very simple way so that you do not need a huge and extensive crystal collection. But there are many books that teach more intricate ways to create a grid. We will work with one central crystal to fit the theme of what you are asking for, and place it in the middle of the grid. We will then surround it with small, single terminator quartz crystals. These will be arranged around the central stone in a circular shape like petals around the centre of a flower.

If you have a history of difficulties with what you would like to manifest, it is worth bearing in mind that you may need to heal and clear before you actually make the grid. For instance, manifesting abundance or a romantic relationship can be very difficult for some people. If this is something you are conscious of, I recommend doing a clearing/healing grid first. This can clear trauma, emotions and mindsets that are sabotaging your ability to manifest. It will also ensure that what you do manifest is of a higher quality.

When creating a clearing/healing grid, place the crystals with their points facing outwards, away from the central stone. This draws out the energies that need to be released from you. Programme the crystal to clear these blocks. Refer to the different lists of crystals suitable for a specific issue. Malachite is a good clearing crystal for self-sabotage, but clear quartz is also a great all-rounder to work with. For a grid created to attract/manifest place the points inwards towards the crystal.

Remember to programme the grid for its chosen intention. Since there are numerous stones, you can try speaking the intention to the stones. Keep the wording clear and direct for best results.

Stones for specific areas of life

Here are different options for the kind of stones you want to use for a grid. Bear in mind that quartz can be used for anything: you programme it with your intention. You don't need to limit yourself to the options given here: these are just suggestions. Go with your intuition.

I suggest keeping a grid out for a week. You can always cleanse the stones and refresh it if you want to continue.

ABUNDANCE

Citrine, tiger's eye, ruby, garnet, gold topaz and nephrite.

I recommend using a large number of single terminator crystals because you are emulating the energy of plenty and multitude. This could also be used with the intention of attracting lots of clients.

BUSINESS

Malachite, aventurine, citrine, tiger's eye, pyrite and lapis lazuli.

More than abundance, a successful business requires focus, endurance, good communication, inspiration and a good sense of timing. Eight single terminators are good for this one because 8 is the number of success, ambition and stability.

LOVE—ATTRACTING A NEW RELATIONSHIP

Rose quartz, larimar, rhodochrosite, emerald, amber, ruby and garnet.

LOVE—ENHANCING AN EXISTING RELATIONSHIP

Fire opal, moonstone, rose quartz, emerald and ruby.

Six is a good number of single terminator crystals for relationships as 6 is the number of the heart and love. It's the number of kindness, empathy and balance.

CREATIVITY

Carnelian, garnet, fire opal, yellow apatite and rainbow fluorite.

This can be done to for general creativity or to assist you with a specific project. Choose the crystal accordingly.

Three single terminators can be good for this one because 3 is the number of creativity and artistic self-expression.

CONFIDENCE

Tiger's eye, citrine, golden topaz and ruby.

Use three single terminators for this one, facing outwards. 3 is the number of confidence, charisma and communication. The pointers face away from the crystal because you want to emulate the energy of expanding your energies outwards to others.

RECOGNITION
Lapis lazuli.

Use 8 single terminator crystals because 8 is the number of professional success.

EMOTIONAL STRENGTH AND STABILITY
Tiger's eye, smoky quartz and nephrite.

This is great for when your emotions are up and down but you also have a lot of chaos in your outer life.

Use 4 terminators to bring a sense of stability, strength and structure.

HEALTH
Citrine, amber, emerald and nephrite – for a general boost to health and vitality. (For specific issues, check the particular healing qualities of each stone.)

Note that when you need a boost or you have a condition that is about a lack of something – e.g. physical energy or iron – then face the stones inwards, towards the stone. But if there is an excess like an infection, inflammation or pain, face the stone outwards to draw these energies away.

Use eight single terminators for this one because 8 is the number of strength and durability.

SERENITY
Blue lace agate, larimar, howlite, lepidolite, selenite.
Use six single terminators for this because 6 is the number of emotional balance and harmony.

PSYCHIC ABILITIES
Nuummite, labradorite, iolite, apophyllite, Herkimer diamond and copper.
Use seven single terminators for this one because 7 is a mystic number.

ATTRACTING FRIENDSHIPS/ SOUL TRIBE
Lapis lazuli, ametrine and rhodocrosite.
Use twelve single terminators if possible because 12 is a powerful number for groups. Think of the 12 apostles and 12 tribes. Otherwise, use six, because 6 is a good number for relating and emotional harmony.

Placement of grids within the home

This is an eight-sided map, which shows the different directions that govern the various areas of life. If possible, place your grid in the relevant side or corner of your home. There are two ways you can use these directions. Either use the front entrance to your home as the bagua map or use the whole home, navigating via the entrance point. The south side of the bagua applies to career and new beginnings, and is mapped at the entrance point of your home.

Personally, my entrance point goes into my living room, and I use the living room only. If you have more than one floor, the ground floor is preferable—but, of course, you need to be practical and consider your own living situation and what will work best.

An example: you are creating a grid to attract a relationship. Place it in the furthest corner to the right of the entrance room, or the furthest to the right corner of the home from the entrance point.

Some of these placements may not be practical for you to use at all. Not to worry: simply use a convenient spot or place on your altar if you have one.

These points are also useful not only for grids but to place a single crystal that fits with the energies of those areas of life for general good energy and attraction.

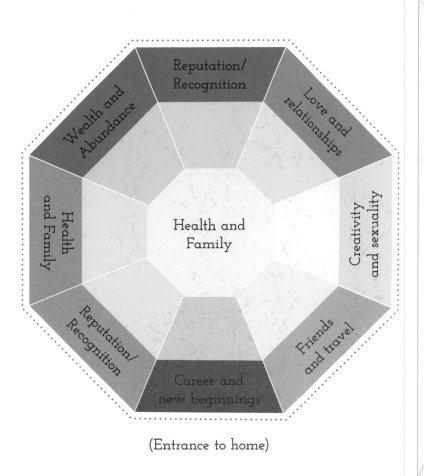

(Entrance to home)

CHAPTER 9
Crystal journeys

A fantastic way to deepen your connection with the Stone People is by journeying. You connect directly to their spirit and receive information organically and personally. There's tonnes of information available about crystals and their various properties and potentials, but nothing can replace learning and receiving through direct experiences and interaction with the spirit.

One way to journey with crystals is with a specific intention and crystal. The interactive experience can reveal a lot and make us more proactive in the healing process.

How to journey

The idea behind journeying is to go into an altered state of consciousness, enabling you to receive information, insight and healing. We can see this in hypnotherapy, shamanic journeying and meditation.

These altered states occur when our brainwave frequencies slow down. In a normal waking state, we are in what is known as the beta state. We are alert, active and able to carry out everyday tasks.

Through journeying practices, we slow down the brain frequencies. These can shift to alpha, theta and delta. This is where we can be more open to receiving

messages from our subconscious and spiritual wisdom, while our repressed emotions can surface and the body can rejuvenate and heal. Theta and delta are states that we go into when sleeping and dreaming. We can also send positive messages to our subconscious mind to change and improve our mindset.

For these journeys, I suggest working with shamanic drumming audios (you can find many for free online. Look for the ones with the callback). Of course, if you have access to live shamanic drumming, that's even better. Alternatively, there are many hertz frequency audios, also available for free online. Hertz frequencies are specific sound frequencies, that are used to create these altered states. Try anything between 15 and 40 minutes. Experiment: some people need more time, some can achieve what they want quickly. It is worth having a notebook handy to record your experiences because the information can disappear from memory quite quickly.

If you are new to this sort of experience, keep an open mind about what you receive. You may be a very visual person or you might instead feel or sense things more; some people hear or see words. Everybody is different and there is no right or wrong. If you feel like you are not receiving much at all, be patient. It can be like training muscles that you haven't used before. You can also use the layout for opening the third eye (see page 113) and work with third eye crystals to help develop and enhance these abilities.

JOURNEY TO MEET A CRYSTAL ALLY

In some shamanic traditions there is what is known as an 'animal spirit ally'. This is an animal that has close affiliations with the person's spirit. It can provide protection and guidance. Its specific behaviour patterns can teach you how to deal with the challenges of a difficult situation.

It is also possible to have a crystal ally. Mine is obsidian, and that became apparent to me through dreams. But another way to find your crystal is through journeying to find one and interact with it.

This crystal will somehow energetically have a link to the nature of your life. It can be a powerful protector and guide just like an animal spirit guide.

So choose your music, lie down in a comfortable place and let's journey!

State your intention to yourself for this journey 3 times:

I am journeying to the crystal realms to meet with my crystal ally.

See/feel yourself standing inside a stone circle structure.

You notice/sense that the ground is opening up for you.

Go down into this opening and find yourself being sucked down into the Earth.

Feel/see yourself going further and further down into the Earth's crust where all crystals are created.

Once you are in the crust, you see/feel yourself to be in a cave-like clearing. One that is full of crystals.

See if there is a crystal or crystalline being appearing, or if you sense its presence.

If yes, confirm that this is your ally. Trust your feelings.

If a crystal being is not obvious to you, ask it what sort of crystal it is.

It may speak to you with words or signs, or you may feel the information.

Take note of the crystal's appearance, in case you need to look it up afterwards.

Introduce yourself as if making a new friend or, in this case, a teacher.

Connect and bond with it.

Ask it what its healing properties are and how it would like to work with you.

Thank it.

See it shrink to the size of your heart and enter you through your heart to become one with you.

When the callback comes or the music is ending, come back up through the Earth back to the stone circle.

Make your notes. If possible, get a piece of this stone physically if you don't already have it. If this is difficult, ask it to work with you through journeys and dreams. If it gave you specific things it wants you to do, try to do them soon to keep the energy and connection flowing.

JOURNEY TO CONNECT WITH A CRYSTAL SPIRIT

This is very similar to the previous journey but is not limited to an ally. It can be for a crystal you have recently acquired and want to get to know and learn more. You can receive quite specific information. It may state a particular preference for how it wants to be cleansed or charged, and how or what to use it for. It may tell you information about your life.

You can also use this to ask which crystal you need to work with most right now. I did this recently and was shown a piece of jewellery that needed charging, which I hadn't realized.

Lie down in a comfortable position.

State your intention to yourself for this journey 3 times:
*I am journeying to the crystal realms – to meet, f*or
example, *with the rose quartz piece I was just given/the
crystal I need to work with right now*

See/feel yourself standing inside a stone circle structure.

You notice/sense that the ground is opening up for you.

Go down into this opening and find yourself being sucked
down into the Earth.

Feel/see yourself going further and further down into the Earth's crust where all crystals are created.

Once you are in the crust, you see/feel yourself to be in some sort of a cave-like clearing. One that is full of crystals.

Wait for your crystal to appear in whatever form it wants to reveal itself.

Enjoy the interaction and be open to whatever this stone spirit wants to impart to you.

Ask it anything you want to ask.

When the callback comes or the music comes to an end, thank it and say goodbye.

Come back up through the Earth to your starting point.

Make notes about your experience and carry out any actions that you were given.

JOURNEY WITH ROSE QUARTZ INTO THE HEART CAVE

This journey is fantastic for bringing us back into our hearts. Often with busy lives and painful emotional experiences, we can cut ourselves off from our hearts and our true emotions. If there is pain in our heart, acknowledging and feeling it will allow it to release.

Gianni Grow's words are pertinent here. 'Grandfather says: "When you feel powerless, it's because you stopped listening to your own heart".' This journey gives us the space to connect and really feel what is inside. We can also see if our inner child needs some comfort and reassurance. The 'inner child' is a term in psychology for the part of our subconscious that picked up emotional and mental messages and social conditioning from before puberty when we were unquestioning and completely susceptible. We carry this with us throughout our lives and it is where early trauma and the roots of certain mindsets are seated. It can be hugely healing to interact with our inner child because this can bring comfort when we experience emotional triggers, and make us less emotionally reactive.

The rose quartz will amplify whatever is in our heart so we can see it more clearly. It also offers comfort, softness, love and a sense that we are not alone.

Lie down in a comfortable position.

Place a piece of rose quartz over your heart.

State your intention to yourself and the crystal 3 times:

I am journeying into my heart centre with this rose quartz to connect with my heart.

Spend a minute just breathing in and out of your heart centre – immersing yourself and bringing your complete attention to this spot.

Feel your chest rise and sink with every breath.

See a swirling vortex opening at your heart centre and go into it.

Journey down and down into your heart cave, spiralling down until you stop and find yourself at a heart-shaped cave entrance.

Step into this entrance and find yourself in a cave illuminated by a pulsating, soft pink light.

You see a child near the entrance. This is your inner child.

How old are they?

Are they happy, sad, angry?

If they need comfort, take them in your arms and ask them what they are feeling and what they want. Tell them what they need to hear—the words you needed to hear as a child. When you are ready, allow these words to dissolve into you.

Feel what is going on in your heart and any experiences that are happening in the cave.

Be open to whatever may arise.

Feel the vibration from the rose quartz interacting with your heart centre.

Receive whatever it is that you need.

When the callback comes or the music starts to end, thank the rose quartz and come back out of the heart cave the way you came.

Make a note of your experience and if there are any actions that you need to carry out.

JOURNEY TO CLEAR ENERGY FROM PREVIOUS SEXUAL PARTNERS WITH ORANGE KYANITE

Every time we have a sexual interaction, we exchange our energies with that person.

These energies can stay with us for years and can have a profound effect on us. Orange kyanite is a powerful tool to clear these energies, freeing us from these influences, which can be draining or confusing to us energetically.

We will be working with the sacral chakra in this journey, which is where we store these energies. This exercise can also be used to release sexual trauma or where the interactions were not always welcome.

Lie down in a comfortable place.

Place the orange kyanite on your sacral chakra. For women, this will be on top of your womb, between the belly button and the pubic bone.

State your intention to yourself and the stone 3 times:

I am journeying into my sacral chakra to release any energy from previous sexual encounters into the orange kyanite.

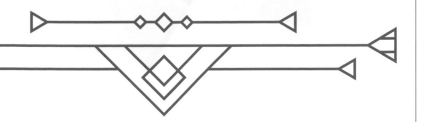

Breathe deep into this area.

Allow your mind to drop into this space.

Feel that you are dropping further down into it.

When you feel settled there, see how you feel.

How does the space feel? Spacious? Heavy or light? Is there any emotion there?

Bring to mind your first sexual partner.

See/feel if their energies are still inside your sacral chakra.

Feel them rising up out of your sexual centre and being absorbed by the crystal. You may feel some residual emotion leaving with the energy.

Tell them that you release them with love.

Do the same process with the next person.

Allow the process to take the time it needs with each

person. Some may be quick, others may need a little more patience.

When the callback comes or the music is ending, thank the kyanite and bring your consciousness out of your sacral chakra and come back to the normal waking state.

One session may be enough for you, or you might need several. It's also worth going back to check in at a later date to see if there are any more energies wanting release. As mentioned before, these energies can stay with us for many years. The interaction of energies, particularly where there has been ongoing involvement over time, can be intense.

CHAPTER 10
Magical baths

M agical baths have been enjoyed by many cultures and spiritual traditions throughout time.

Here, as you may have guessed, we will be using crystal-infused waters, but also essential oils and flowers. Use your intuition to guide you and create your own baths for healing and enjoyment.

The crystal water infusion

To make the crystal water infusion for any bath, take your chosen crystal and cleanse it. Then place it in a glass container or bottle. Fill it up with 250–500ml of water – mineral, distilled or (if you have access) drinkable water from a fresh, natural source.

Cover and leave for 6–12 hours.

A NOTE ABOUT ESSENTIAL OILS

Always dilute essential oils with a carrier oil, otherwise they can be too strong for the skin. Proportion and carrier oil recommendations will be listed. Most essential oils are not suitable for use by pregnant women or children under six. But you can always refer to lists of contraindications on websites created by qualified aromatherapists. Always do a skin test to check that you don't have an allergy or sensitivity to any of the ingredients for these baths.

Smell is also extremely personal, so always follow your nose about what most appeals.

Simple bathing and showering is actually one of the most effective ways to cleanse, not only our body but our energetic field. But with the added effect of plants, magical intention and crystalline vibration, we can turn this into a magical ritual. Prepare for a treat!

The baths

After you get out of the bath, it is better not to rub yourself down with a towel so that you can keep the plant and crystal essences on your body to absorb even more of their benefits. Just gently dab yourself dry or, better still, let yourself dry in the air.

CLEARING QUARTZ BATH

This bath is great for clearing our energies. Quartz also amplifies our auric field, giving us a more expansive feeling and a clearer mind. The white and the essential oils are soothing for the spirit.

1 quartz crystal, for the infusion

250–500 ml (8–16 fl oz, 2 cups) milk (cow's or coconut)

white flowers (such as rose, carnation or freesia)

7 drops of benzoin, frankincense or white lotus oil mixed in 2 teaspoons (10ml) sweet almond or grapeseed oil.

Run the bath and add all the ingredients.

Take the crystal-infused water and pour it into the bath.

Speak or blow an intention into the water three times.

Get in and enjoy!

For maximum effect, make sure your head and face make contact with the water.

Spend at least 10 minutes in this bath to really soak up the benefits.

REVITALIZING GARNET BATH

This bath is great for energizing us and giving us a pickup when we feel we have lost our mojo or passion, or we feel downtrodden. It can enhance our magnetism, so if we want to feel on top of our game and are wishing to attract romantically or professionally, this is a good choice.

1 garnet crystal, for the infusion

750 ml (25 fl oz, 3 cups) rose water

7 drops rose oil, ylang ylang or patchouli oil diluted in 2 teaspoons (10ml) sweet almond or grapeseed oil

red flowers (such as red roses or red freesia)

Run the bath and add all the ingredients.

Take the crystal-infused water and pour it into the bath with everything else in there.

Speak or blow an intention into the water three times.

Get in and enjoy!

For maximum effect, make sure your head and face make contact with the water.

Spend at least 10 minutes in this bath to really soak up the benefits.

SUNNY CITRINE BATH

This is a wonderful bath for uplifting the spirits, clearing the mind and any fatigue.

1 citrine crystal, for the infusion

2 tablespoons honey

Yellow flowers (such as rose, freesia or carnation)

7 drops may chang essential oil or rosemary (note that this is not suitable for epileptics), blended in 2 teaspoons (10ml) sweet almond or grapeseed oil

Run the bath and add all the ingredients.

Take the crystal-infused water and pour it into the bath with everything else in there.

Speak or blow an intention into the water three times.

Get in and enjoy!

For maximum effect, make sure your head and face make contact with the water.

Spend at least 10 minutes in this bath to really soak up the benefits.

DREAMTIME AMETHYST BATH

Treat yourself to this bath if you are stressed, anxious or having difficulty sleeping. It helps you to unwind and relax, especially just before going to bed. The amethyst can also help you to have sweet dreams.

1 amethyst crystal, for the infusion

7 drops lavender essential oil (add 1 drop valerian oil for an extra potent mix), diluted in 2 teaspoons sweet almond or grapeseed oil

Purple flowers (such as freesias and/or lavender)

Take the crystal-infused water and pour it into the bath.

Speak or blow an intention into the water three times.

Get in and enjoy!

For maximum effect, make sure your head and face make contact with the water.

Spend at least 10 minutes in this bath to really soak up the benefits.

Index

Further reading

Ahsan, Hamraz *The Essential Book of Auras* (Arcturus Publishing, 2020).

Asar, Justin Moikeha *Liquid Crystal Oracle* (Blue Angel Publishing, 2010).

Bourgault, Luc *The American Indian secrets of Crystal Healing* (Quantum Publishing, 1992).

Gienger, Michael *Healing Crystals: The A–Z guide to 555 Gemstones* (Earth Dancer, 2005).

Hall, Judy *101 Power Crystals: The Ultimate Guide to Magical Crystals, Gems, and Stones for Healing and Transformation* (Fair Winds Press, 2011).

Kok Sui, Master Choa *Pranic Crystal Healing* (Institute for Inner Studies Publishing Foundation, 1996).

Raphaell, Katrina *Crystal Enlightenment: The Transforming Properties of Crystals and Healing Stones* (Aurora Press, 1986).